In the same series:

surfing, grégory maubé – sylvain cazenave

skateboarding, fabrice le mao – mathias fennetaux

kitesurfing, marc bory

© Fitway Publishing 2005
Original editions in French, English, Spanish, Italian

All rights reserved, including partial or complete translation, adaptation and
reproduction rights in any form and for any purpose.

Translation by Translate-A-Book, Oxford

Design and creation: GRAPH'M/Nord Compo, France

ISBN: 2-7528-0124-6
Publisher code: T00124

Copyright registration: October 2005
Printed in Italy by Rotolito Lombarda

www.fitwaypublishing.com

Fitway Publishing – 12 avenue d'Italie – 75627 Paris cedex 13, France

extreme **S**ports

snowboarding

patricia oudit

fitway.
publishing

contents

The Snowboard Revolution

Snowboarding may look dangerous and far-out, but nothing could be more natural: to slide downhill and stop by simply turning side-on. Sounds straightforward? It is …

Snowboarding has made its mark on other disciplines. Before the advent of the snowboard, skis were two metres long; once snowboarding came on the scene, skis became shorter, more manageable, parabolic. Before the snowboard, we had gates and timed runs for the pros and prepared *pistes* for the weekend skier; post-snowboard came powder and freedom of choice for everyone. The whole mountain was up for grabs. We were free to snowboard when and where we liked, shoot hair-raising videos, converse in boarding slang and franglais, and hurt wrists rather than knees. It was fun to wear the baggy pants, dress grunge-style and act cool and laid-back.

For some people, snowboarding is more than a game, however: it is a way of life. Back in 1985, snowboard pioneer Régis Rolland claimed that skiing was serious whereas snowboarding was all fun and games – *and* somewhat less elitist, one might add. Twenty years on, however, everything has changed. Snow sports have been democratised and the bottom line now is to give people what they want. Despite what its detractors may say, there was life before snowboarding and there will be life after. Régis was right – standing sideways, sliding on a little board *was* fun. But it also pointed the way towards a whole range of Third Millennium winter sports.

Axel Pauporte carries the day at X-treme 2000 in Verbier. Snowboarding epitomises a new and, at times, disconcerting sense of freedom that has made conventional snow addicts think again …

Genesis

Whose **Crazy Idea** Was **This?**

Recent excavations reveal that *homo surfus* first emerged on Planet Earth towards the end of the 1920s, when young Americans started to fashion crude boards from wooden barrels in a bid to relieve the boredom of periods when the surf was not 'up'. Recent research has also shown that the first embryonic snowboard was the brainchild of M.J. 'Jack' Burchett, who built himself a plywood board and bound it with strips of cloth and leather reins. 'Snowsurfing' (as the sport was known for a long time before our American friends came up with the term 'snowboarding') was first and foremost a matter of ingenious do-it-yourself improvisation. It was not until the 1960s that the sport started to take off in earnest, when a few pioneering prophets took to the snow-covered backyards of North America. Thirteen-year-old Tom Sims, miffed at not being able to skate in the Californian winter, pestered one of his teachers to design a board capable of hurtling down a *piste*. Tom would go on to greater things: a few years later, he and his buddy Chuck Barfoot set up Sims Snowboards, working out of the family garage, putting together their Flying Yellow Banana – a plastic board with roller-skate add-ons. Along came Sherman Popper, to whom we are indebted for the 'snurfer' ('snow' + 'surf'), a twin-ski assembly originally designed as a sledge for his young daughter. Then, in the early 1970s, East Coast surfer Dimitri Milovich pushed the envelope by designing a prototype board complete with dorsal fin and swallow tail: the legendary Winterstick.

Old-fashioned ways … and some sample bindings from way back when. For the snowboard pioneers of 1970–1980, swallow-tail boards were the order of the day …

French snowboard pioneer Henri Authier wasn't convinced by the Winterstick prototype when he first clapped eyes on it during a competition in Salt Lake City. His initial reaction was that this hybrid was fit for use only in powder: 'All kinds of new ski fads like acrobatics and monoski were hitting the headlines back then,' says Authier, 'so no one figured this contraption would ever catch on'. Nevertheless, he brought the new board over to France in the late 1970s and decided to give it a whirl in the marketplace. 'I went to see Barlan, who was producing kitesurf boards in the south of France at the time. He had his doubts and I pulled the plug on the whole the idea. How's that for missing out?' These early and, at times, madcap ideas all pointed in one direction – developing a device that would float on snow in much the same way as a surfboard skims the water. The Holy Grail was that sublime feeling of 'weightlessness'. And the road to perfection would lead through innumerable prototypes and customised boards tried out in the 1970s. The big question – the *existential* question, more like – was how to keep one's feet on the board rather than fly head over heels into the scenery every few seconds. Aluminium fins were mooted and the first spoilers were mounted. And some weird and comical shapes appeared in the powder: New Age surfers kitted out in moon boots or hiking shoes, tied on with nylon cords or strips cut from inner tubes, clutching a kind of leash attached to the front end of the board in the vain hope of steering it …

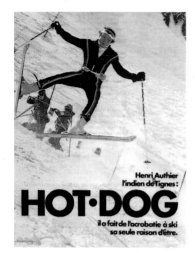

Henri Authier
l'indien de Tignes:

HOT·DOG

il a fait de l'acrobatie à ski
sa seule raison d'être.

Above: *Henri Authier (call sign 'Indian') made his mark as a hot-dogger before nailing the first Winterstick competition in France.*

Right: *Exploiting the terrain and diving (literally) into powder.*

Henri Authier in action on his prototype finboard imported from the USA. An article penned in 1979 by Gilles Chappaz offers one of the earliest descriptions of the new and unique sensation of 'floating' in powder ...

The Founding Fathers
of Modern Snowboarding

Come the late 1970s and early 1980s, a whole legion of people could lay claim to have contributed some small detail or other to snowboard design, but there were precious few who had a genuine vision, let alone an inkling of how it might best be commercialised. In terms of equipment development, Jake Burton was one of the few who did. Régis Rolland was another.

Jake Burton:
Gentleman Snowboarder *par excellence*

Jake Burton Carpenter, the world's first-ever commercial snowboard manufacturer, has laboured long and hard for three decades to promote snowboarding as a sport, without sacrificing its ethos. He is in his fifties now, but the smile is as naively engaging as ever, the eyes frank and uncalculating. Self-taught snowboarder Burton would rather be carving the powder than ploughing through the accounts: 'They tell me I have a 35% share of the snowboard market,' he says modestly, looking down at the floor like a naughty schoolboy. Deliberately self-effacing? Perhaps. But one prefers to believe that this is Jake Burton's way of persuading himself that he hasn't swapped his youthful enthusiasm for the more sedate life of a businessman.

Burton needn't worry. The snowboarding world is unlikely to forget the flair and commitment shown by a callow 14-year-old who developed his youthful passion for his 'snurfer' and eventually translated it into big bucks.

Left: *Jake Burton thrives on competition. When snowboarding made its Olympic debut in 1998, he promised a bonus to those members of his team who were less than up for it.*

Right-hand page: *Burton's Theory of Snowboard Evolution – from inner tube to modern board design and from minimalist decoration to advanced graphics.*

Jake Burton in his plastic boots. A far cry from
his early days as a seven-year-old downhiller
and well before he committed to snowboarding.

'I was a fresh-faced kid at the time,' recalls Burton. 'And like every other kid on the block I used to horse around on a fifteen-dollar toy. Back then, *nobody* figured snowboarding would catch on, me included.'

That said, Burton took the plunge in 1977, deciding to set up a snowboard workshop on the strength of a windfall inheritance. Things didn't pan out and Jake went through one hundred thousand dollars: 'I was flat broke. On my own, no one working for me. I did everything myself, sawing and gluing with my own two hands, then doing trial runs on the slope behind my place.' Between round trips to the hardware store, Burton somehow found time to show his maple boards in Las Vegas – side by side with the Winterstick. That was the breakthrough he needed. He sold three hundred boards in 1979. This initial success had its downside, as his wife Donna, who now runs Jake's marketing and distribution business, recalls: 'The garage was too small to store all his stuff, which was taking over everywhere. The barn was his production facility, our office was in the dining room, the lounge was our showroom, and the kids were like strangers. They used to call Jake on the house phone at two in the morning and he'd say something like "please leave your name and address and I'll get back to you" …'

Since those early years, Jake has come to be regarded as the 'pope of snow-boarding'. He was the brains behind the US Open, the first snowboarding competition of the modern era. An exemplary family man and father of three, Jake Burton is light years away from the joint-smoking, beer-swilling aficionados who worshipped at his feet. Fact is, Jake likes nothing better than breathing in the healthy mountain air that caresses the slopes of Burlington, Vermont (where his production plant is now located): 'When the snow is good, I go out riding with a few of the guys,' he says.

In 2003–2004, Jake took his family on a worldwide snowboarding tour. Taking to the road Kerouac-style was Jake's way of thumbing his nose at competitors who have been snapping at his heels for years. 'The ski manufacturers waited too long before getting into the market,' he points out. 'Unlike them, we are now able to plough a major chunk of our profits back into research.'

For all its popularity, the world of snowboarding is a curiously close-knit community and Jake Burton knows who is who and what is what. Besides, he has never stopped promoting the sport, although he has been careful not to add fuel to the fires of controversy that rage between snowboarders and skiers. 'I am a snow-skier myself,' says Jake, 'and I have great respect for the sport. Snowboarding was attacked by people who claimed we would screw up the powder. Not so. But convincing US ski resorts to develop snow parks and half-pipes was anything but easy.' Quite. But it was Burton's 'Free the Snow' campaign that finally persuaded die-hards that snowboarders had come of age and were no longer the much-maligned dropouts and tearaways of yesteryear.

Jake Burton is committed to teaching people how to snowboard and, more importantly, how to have fun doing it. His 'Learn to Ride' centres for beginners are a case in point: 'The idea is to keep folks from snowboarding until they've mastered the basics. The better they ride, the more fun they'll have. And the less dangerous the sport will become for themselves and for other people.'

In the interim, Jake Burton, missionary *extraordinaire*, has set up a foundation to teach snowboarding to kids from underprivileged backgrounds. As Jake Burton sees it, everyone has the right to make his mark. Not only literally but also metaphorically …

Burton never claimed to have invented snowboarding. He acknowledges that the board he is riding in this photo is the brainchild of one Vern Micklund, which featured in a recently rediscovered video dating back to 1939.

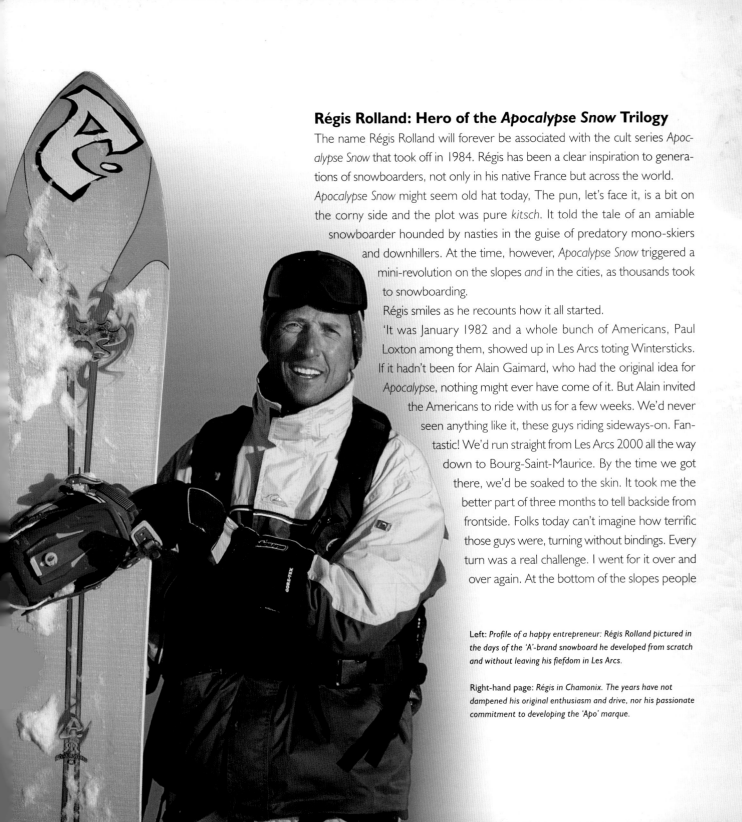

Régis Rolland: Hero of the *Apocalypse Snow* Trilogy

The name Régis Rolland will forever be associated with the cult series *Apocalypse Snow* that took off in 1984. Régis has been a clear inspiration to generations of snowboarders, not only in his native France but across the world. *Apocalypse Snow* might seem old hat today, The pun, let's face it, is a bit on the corny side and the plot was pure *kitsch*. It told the tale of an amiable snowboarder hounded by nasties in the guise of predatory mono-skiers and downhillers. At the time, however, *Apocalypse Snow* triggered a mini-revolution on the slopes *and* in the cities, as thousands took to snowboarding.

Régis smiles as he recounts how it all started.

'It was January 1982 and a whole bunch of Americans, Paul Loxton among them, showed up in Les Arcs toting Wintersticks. If it hadn't been for Alain Gaimard, who had the original idea for *Apocalypse*, nothing might ever have come of it. But Alain invited the Americans to ride with us for a few weeks. We'd never seen anything like it, these guys riding sideways-on. Fantastic! We'd run straight from Les Arcs 2000 all the way down to Bourg-Saint-Maurice. By the time we got there, we'd be soaked to the skin. It took me the better part of three months to tell backside from frontside. Folks today can't imagine how terrific those guys were, turning without bindings. Every turn was a real challenge. I went for it over and over again. At the bottom of the slopes people

Left: Profile of a happy entrepreneur: Régis Rolland pictured in the days of the 'A'-brand snowboard he developed from scratch and without leaving his fiefdom in Les Arcs.

Right-hand page: Régis in Chamonix. The years have not dampened his original enthusiasm and drive, nor his passionate commitment to developing the 'Apo' marque.

just stood around, gaping. They couldn't believe their eyes. I guess some of them thought it was just another gimmick. But there I was, with my Bataille boots held on with elastic luggage straps. In my element.'

Régis featured in Alain Gaimard's initial snowboarding movie, *Ski Espace*, shot in 1982 to publicise the new ski resort of Les Arcs.

Snowboarding was captured on celluloid for the first time ever. The opening film in the *Apocalypse* trilogy was shot the following year. It was a hit worldwide and 24-year-old ski instructor and intrepid white-water rafter Régis Rolland was catapulted into iconic status. That was merely the tip of the iceberg. By 1984, it seemed everyone was hard at it, shaping boards and comparing notes. Marques such as DEA, Bird Surf, Adrenaline and Déclic flourished and Eric Gros, head honcho at Hawaii Surf, one of the very first snowboard pro shops in Europe, started marketing his incredible assembly (in real wood, no less). Elsewhere, Hot's Serge Dupraz launched his brilliant wasp-waist board, which enabled six-metre curves and prefigured parabolic ski design.

All the while, Régis Rolland cut a lone figure, a solitary rider plying his trade in Les Arcs ('a real test-bed for new techniques') and wrestling with the biggest and most controversial issue of the day: should the snowboarder's feet be fixed or not? Régis experimented with foot-strap bindings, convinced that 'French' snowboarding, unlike its American counterpart, had its roots not in surfing or skateboarding but in kitesurfing as practised in and around the Mediterranean. Régis was unremitting in his efforts to explore snowboarding's full powder potential, even to the point of riding without spoilers or edges until 1987. 'I quickly learned how to adapt the downhiller's technique of jump turns while still heading straight down,' he recalls. 'That gave the Yanks something to think about,' he adds, with a nod of acknowledgment in the direction of those who started it all off in the first place.

Régis Rolland has since had his ups and downs on the business front but, today, he is happy and secure in his role as the main man at Apo. The 'master' now rides purely for the hell of it – 'I still get a terrific kick out of fresh powder' – but he is deadly serious when it comes to communicating his enthusiasm and passion for the sport to those eager to take it up for the first time.

The Walk. *Snowshoes on, the snowboarder will walk for several hours if there is the remotest prospect of a long run in top-grade powder, ideally – for the pros at any rate – sprinkled with big jumps across exposed rocks. Some marques (including Nitro and Fanatic) seem to find the walk/snowboard combination unappealing and have devised boards that double as cross-country skis …*

Freedom. *It's a great feeling, unique almost, heading off with a light board tucked under one arm. But that's only a foretaste. The real freedom comes when you are out there on the snow, baggies and all, in tune with the elements, the silence punctuated only by the crisp crunch of snow under your board.*

Snowboard
Buzzwords

Powder. *Snowboard caviar. Icing on the cake. The Holy Grail of weightlessness. Snowboarding was made for powder and thrives on it. It is thanks to snowboarding – no, because of snowboarding – that virgin snow, that rarest and most precious of commodities, has been opened up to the hoi polloi. But you have to be an early bird if you want to carve a trail – a really early bird! – and you have to be ready to suggest to others that they move on and find their own deep powder elsewhere.*

The Drop. *Snowboarders walk when they have to, but they also like to fly or, strictly speaking, ride helicopters and set down delicately on a powder-rich summit. There's no problem with this in many countries – from the USA to Russia by way of New Zealand – but it has caused a ruckus in Europe, where many Alpine countries have vetoed it, Italy being one exception.*

Tripping. *Snowboarders take this seriously. There are 'spots' out there everywhere in the world, just waiting to be discovered. Snowboarders are in a constant state of migratory flux, searching for new corners of the globe to check out snow conditions. Like their surfer brethren, they travel in pick-up trucks and live in improvised squats with modest creature comforts. 'Snow bums' and 'surf bums' have this in common: next to no cash but a pocketful of dreams and a season that never ends.*

Line. *The virgin slope. A blank page ready to receive your signature, as the ads would have it. The purer the line, the more intense the sensation. This is the point at which snowboarding most closely resembles surfing.*

Video. *Hirsute yetis and pink rabbits plugged into portable cassette players and, latterly, DVDs. Adolescent and post-adolescent snowboarders partying until very late. Tricks and moves discussed over a couple of beers and mentally rehearsed for the morrow. Catching all this on video provides one of the rare opportunities for riders and sponsors to interface. At least one excellent full-length, straight-to-video production hits the shelves every year. And then there's video gaming, a particular favourite among beginners who can snowboard at will without risking life or limb …*

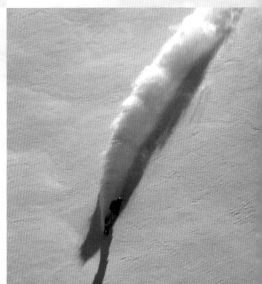

Design **Factors**

Bindings tend to be a bigger issue than the board proper and designing them has spawned all manner of internecine squabbles and backbiting. The early 'official' bindings were securely anchored rigid ('hard') baseplates that also worked with conventional ski boots. The mid-1980s saw the emergence of strip (lanyard) bindings with hooks to receive soft boots; it was goodbye forever to the chafed heels and blistered toes caused by those earlier instruments of torture. Nowadays, the foot nestles snugly inside the boot, shielded against cold and bruising. The boots also make for comfortable après-ski wear. All of this is extremely good news for the truly dedicated snowboarder, for whom the binding/boot combination represents a clear line of demarcation between snowboarding and downhill skiing. Today, baseplates are used exclusively for alpine snowboarding and by riders of the 'old school' who are hooked on carving. Manufacturers have meanwhile come up with a whole new range of bindings, including step-ins (automatic systems where the boot is clamped flat to the baseplate). These have the advantage of enabling the snowboarder to boot up from a standing position. The 'flow' system, on the other hand, comprises a plastic insert into which the boot is clipped toe-first. When all is said and done, however, the loose binding system remains by far the most popular worldwide.

Simple nylon straps were poor relations of footstraps. The straps were used in conjunction with flexible footwear to provide a modicum of comfort and keep the rider's feet secured to the board.

Snowboard **Bandits**

The latter half of the 1980s was chaos, anarchy even. Everybody hankered after the be-all-and-end-all: riding in competition. Parallel circuits featuring slalom and mogul runs were all the rage – and tough on boards designed for carving through powder! The first-ever snowboarding world championships were held in Europe, in Livigno (Italy) and St. Moritz (Switzerland). In the alpine category, podium places went to France's Jean Nerva, Mylène Duclos, Ian Giauchain, Dédé Maszewski, Serge Vitelli, Eric Rey and Denis Bertrand; to Germany's Peter Bauer and to the Swiss trio of José Fernandes, Antoine Massy and Philippe Imhof. The United States had already switched over to freestyle by this time, with frontliners like Terry Kidwell (the 'daddy of freestyle'), Craig Kelly and Mike Jacoby, who executed 540°s (one-and-a-half full twists while airborne). Moves like that dumbfounded European snowboarders but, at the same time, were an inspiration to addicts like Bert Lamar, who would pass into snowboarding legend on account of his celebrated Look Lamar board specifically designed for 'grabbing' (catching hold of the end of the board with either hand while airborne). There is little prospect of snowboarding knocking downhill skiing off its pedestal, but snowboarders are entitled to dream the dream. That said, snowboarding's detractors were quick off the mark. The snowboarder is *persona non grata* at a number of US winter-sports resorts, which look down their noses at the rough-and-ready snowboarding fraternity as they might at a dangerous new species. This an attitude that persists in four resorts in Utah, New Mexico and Vermont. Europe also went into culture shock, albeit to a lesser degree. The arch-conservative downhillers tended to regard these oddball 'snow surfers' with what can best be described as benign scepticism and, from time to time, gatemen turn snowboarders away on the grounds that their boards are liable to damage the ski-lifts.

Left-hand page: *Snowboarding democratised powder and, in the process, scared ski resort officialdom everywhere. The initial reaction was to ban the new discipline, but times have changed …*

Below: *The madcap years of zinc and fluorescence, when 'snow-surfers' were regarded as iconoclasts at best and, at worst, as a horde of godless outlaws.*

Some resorts have got around this by obliging snowboarders to lug mini-skis on their backs before using the lifts. In several European resorts, a leash is mandatory and the would-be 'board-blockers' delight in recounting horror stories of runaway boards hurtling down black runs and putting downhiller lives at risk.

Some resorts have shrugged off this negative attitude, however, and have greenlighted the sport. As of 1989, Europe took a leaf out of the US book and started to install halfpipes. The Swiss, with snow parks in Saas-Fée and Laax, and the Austrians, notably in the Tyrol, are out front in this respect, and France is gradually sitting up and taking notice, as witness developments in Les Arcs, Avoriaz, Serre-Chevalier and Les Deux-Alpes, the venue for the first-ever snowboarding world championships in 1989. A modest number of equipment suppliers have erected stalls 3,200 metres (10,500 feet) up on the glacier and these attract hundreds of connoisseurs daily. To date, some fifteen thousand would-be snowboarders have made the trek to try out – for free – the wide range of equipment on offer.

The Mad Years

Sales **Spiral**, Tensions **Mount** …

By the early 1990s, snowboarding was already big business. Board sales climbed to hundreds of thousands worldwide (exceeding 800,000 in the winter of 1995–1996 alone) and some four hundred different board marques were on the market. In Japan, where tradition and novelty exist side by side, the market expanded exponentially. Until then, the Japanese marketplace had been serviced by a large number of lesser-known brands, but the Big Guns – who had previously bet their shirts on downhill skiing – recognised the potential and quickly got into the action. Elsewhere, the first pro teams were appearing on the scene, headed by perennial snowboarders Peter Bauer and Jean Nerva from the Burton stable. Burton's 'girls' included Norway's Ashild Loftus, who racked up alpine titles, while Switzerland's Nicole Angelrath scooped the freestyle category. In double-quick time, the snowboarding world was jam-packed with big names such as the American, Peter Line, an inveterate inventor of tricks and moves, France's cutting-edge boarder, David Vincent, or the multi-talented Norwegian free spirit, Terje Haakonsen. Freestyle aficionados were making their presence felt with a vengeance and the phoney war between alpine riders and freestyle 'new-schoolers' was hotting up. The latter were destined to win out. In the United States, the alpine traditionalists had already been eclipsed: alpine equipment sales fell away to a modest 5% market share in 1993. Switzerland's Bertie Denervaud was one of the few snowboarders to keep a foot in both camps. In the final analysis, it didn't really matter. The main thing was that snowboarding had come out of its ghetto and was now well and truly on the map. In the United States, the urbanite craze was for competitions ('contests') and 'summer camps', whereas Europe dragged its heels until Innsbruck and the first-ever freestyle extravaganza, the aptly named 'Air & Style' of 1993. That same year in France, Fred Beauchêne

(the king of indoor surfing) customised the Trocadéro as a parallel slalom *piste*. The potential financial rewards were there for all to see and everybody wanted a slice of the cake, not least the International Snowboarding Federation (ISF) which successfully rallied the troops with the stick-and-carrot prospect of Winter Olympics action. Snowboarders started appearing with increasing frequency in TV commercials, where images of the streetwise city-dweller vs. the clean-living lad from the mountains were judiciously permutated, depending on the product the advertisers wanted to move, be it an automobile or a box of breakfast cereal. Scores of snowboarding magazines appeared on the newsstands and bombarded an adolescent public with controversial photos of a new, exciting and dangerous sport.

Left-hand page: *In 1993 tons of snow were trucked into the Trocadéro by Fred Beauchêne for the first-ever urban snowboarding show – to the utter amazement of the Parisian public.*

Above: *Serge Vitelli and the entire Quiksilver team on the Brévent summit in Chamonix during a successful snowboarding session full of non-stop action and lifestyle affirmation …*

Faux **Rebels** but Dedicated
Followers of Fashion ...

Below: *As 'baggy' as it gets: gravity takes over as outsize trousers slowly but inexorably start to sag. Note the belt (clearly for decorative purposes only).*

Right-hand page: *Changing snowboarding fashions: a hint of fluo, a touch of pastel and a dash of scarlet set off the obligatory 'baggy'.*

Arguably the most remarkable phenomenon in terms of the snowboarding boom has been the spectacular surge in sales of snow wear and accessories. There is no getting away from it: the archetypal snowboarder, barely out of his or her teens, comes as a rule from a comparatively well-off background and is a dedicated follower of fashion, not to say a fashion victim. And, since the fashions in question typically have a single-season shelf life, 'grunge' gear designers and manufacturers have quickly zeroed in on a new cash cow, targeting a burgeoning and well-heeled clientele where, it would seem, 'trash means cash'.

Over the years, snow gear has evolved, often to the verge of caricature. Highlights of the interminable fashion parade include the aluminium and fluorescent styles that were definitely 'in' back in the 1980s, when flashy jumpsuits favoured by the mono-ski fraternity were customised into body-hugging versions accessorised by headbands and over-the-top shades. Come the 1990s, baseball caps were worn – *de rigueur* backwards – to set off mountaineering-style pullovers or fleeces; ski-pants featured decorative protective patches; and gimmicky accessories included three-finger ski mitts. The latter half of the 1990s was all baggies and XXL, but first and foremost it was an explosion of colour. The sacrosanct woollen ski-cap, rescued from years of oblivion, ceded pride of place to garish red and platinum-blonde hair or to Rasta dreadlocks. Metal was in vogue, with rapper-style rings on every finger, and ears, noses, eyebrows, navels and whatever duly pierced. Tattoos were, of course, mandatory. The new millennium then saw a throwback to the 1970s and the Age of Punk: chunky belts and studded arm bracelets were dusted off. Baggies, as ever, are worn 'loose and low', in exaggerated hipster mode, with knee-length crotch and G-string on show. Chain-mail woven headgear has made a comeback, as have the woollen cap, complete with brim, and outsize fleece-lined jackets and hoods.

Bipeds vs. Dwarfs with ski-caps

Above: *Snowboarders and skiers alike take to wearing knitted, Peruvian, pompom-style or visor bonnets, bridging the gap between the two disciplines.*

Right-hand page: *The war of words between snowboarders and skiers dragged on for a few seasons, with each side arguing its case. Ultimately, common sense prevailed as the two sides gradually came to realise they had more in common than they at first believed.*

When the baggy-trousered and ski-cap-wearing 'dwarfs' appeared *en masse* on the slopes in the mid-1990s — so-called because of their tendency to sit or squat in the snow — they sparked off a phoney war with the 'bipeds' (conventional downhillers), who were aghast at the prospect of their precious two-footer territory being veritably swamped by a barbarian *tsunami*.

By this time, of course, snowboarding had gone truly international and youngsters everywhere were flocking to the sport — even adolescent Muscovites, who snowboarded in the cities. This posed a major problem for winter sports resorts, which now had to choose between sticking to their traditional ways or jumping on this new and self-evidently lucrative bandwagon. The plain fact was that, in the space of a few years, a whole new generation had taken to the slopes, kids and young adults who had never skied before and knew next to nothing about the mountains and how to behave there. They were city kids in the main, usually with skateboarding backgrounds; kids who didn't give a damn about the locals and their safety-conscious attitudes. They horsed around at the lifts or in the cabins and carried on like characters from the *South Park* comic strip or lobotomised adolescents straight out of *Wayne's World*. Predictably, these were the fall guys whose habits and attitudes were heavily and indiscriminately criticised. Generalisations flew thick and fast: snowboarders were to blame for anything and everything, all the way from causing avalanches to indulging in acts of vandalism.

Above: *The Salomon snowboard squad living it up like schoolchildren on an RV road trip taking in various French resorts.*

Right-hand page: *Learning the basics before venturing up the mountain: knees bent, arms extended, eyes fixed on the horizon to help maintain balance and orientation.*

They were binge drinkers who wrecked the place, squatted parking lots and were pushy at chair lifts. In other words, they were all tarred with the same brush. Before long, the generally low esteem in which they were held spawned a reaction that reached epidemic proportions in some countries. That's what happened in the United States and France, two countries where snowboarding had made major breakthroughs. In the United States, snow patrols were more militant than ever, quite prepared even to throw snowboarders into jail without a second thought. In France, vigilance was stepped up and security measures became increasingly strict. A plethora of bans and prohibitions followed and self-righteous editorialising was the order of the day, to the point where ex-world champion skier Marielle Goitschel was pilloried in the snowboarding press.

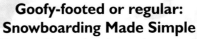

Goofy-footed or regular:
Snowboarding Made Simple

The success enjoyed by snowboarding can be summed up in one word: accessibility. It's said that it takes eight years to learn to ski and eight days to learn to snowboard. That said, it was some time before the first genuine snowboard instructors appeared. One obvious explanation may be that snowboarding basics were so easy to teach that there was not enough work to go around; another is that some avid beginners take at most a few days before they are as good as or better than their instructors. Self-taught snowboarders know how easy it all is, that it takes perhaps only a day and a half to make sure one doesn't acquire bad habits. Over the last few years, however, schools have sprung up right, left and centre, offering courses geared to specific disciplines such as freeride or freestyle. The fact that formal study courses are already being offered in some schools is a sure-fire sign that the sport is rapidly becoming formally acknowledged and institutionalised.

Movers and Shapers

The 'shaper' is the main man as far as snowboarding practitioners and competitors are concerned. *Piste* preparation and the stopwatch used to be the most important things but, these days, it's all about parks, areas and zones. Forget about timing runs down to the last hundredth of a second – the emphasis is now exclusively on *style*. Fact is, snowboarding has revolutionised the whole snow sports scene by importing streetwise urban 'attitude'. A whole new generation is calling the shots and the resorts have had to come up with the goods …

Snow Parks on Parade

Big Air: The rider takes off from a three- to ten-metre-high ramp that 'kicks' him up some three metres into the air. He lands anything up to twenty metres away. While airborne, he performs a trick. If the landing area is not sufficiently steep, the jump is known as a 'heel-buster'.

Quarter/Hip: The rider hits a comparatively steep take-off ramp and climbs high, executing a quarter-twist before dropping straight down on the landing area. This is a more difficult figure than 'Big Air', since the edges are needed for take-off.

Whoops: A series of larger moguls arranged in twos. The rider takes them on one at a time or clears both at once. If his run-up is too slow, he can generate additional speed by loading the board on the downside slope of the whoop.

Step-Up: Where the landing area is above the take-off point on the ramp (which can be up to five metres high). Unlike the classic downhill variant, the rider has to climb ('step up') to land the jump successfully.

Gap: A ten to fifteen-metre space between take-off ramp and landing area. If a rider is too slow on his approach he runs the risk of wiping out.

Handrail: Ramp used by a rider to perform 'slides'. A single-turn ramp is called a 'C-rail', a double-turn curving left and right is an 'S', and an ascending and descending ramp is known as a 'rainbow'.

Fun Box: A long box, made of plastic or metal, on which the rider performs a trick figure.

The Age of Reason

Infinite **Permutations …**

By the end of the 1990s, the early squabbles had abated, although certain large resorts continue to take a hard line. Snowboarding has come of age and with age comes respectability. The sport made its Olympic debut in Nagano, Japan in 1998 and millions were able to see then that snowboarding had its rightful place among other high-end sports. By the turn of the century, there had been a substantive shift in attitude. The winter sports resorts granted absolution to the snowboarding sinners and, by the same token, a certain number of seasoned snowboarders reverted to downhill without being branded as traitors to the snowboarding cause. At the same time, however, the purists who had voiced fears that the very ethos of snowboarding was being sacrificed on the altar of competition and commercial interest were, to some extent, proved right. Over the years, sponsorship priorities have evolved to the point where some pro riders are little more than advertising hoardings in a sport where 'freedom' and 'individualism' were once the watchwords.

It should be added, however, that such developments do not affect the vast majority. Snowboarders and downhillers rarely clash on the *piste* or off it. They ski in parallel now, whether on boards or parabolic skis. Freestyle and freeride reign supreme these days. The snowboarder is a 'zapper' who switches styles and rides at the drop of a hat, enjoying other high-adrenaline sports – in the air (base-jumping from cliffs), on the water (kayaking downriver) or even on tarmac (skateboarding). Whatever, the only difference between pros and dedicated amateurs is one of degree in terms of performance and the relative level of inherent risk.

Left: *'Look, Ma, I'm flying!' The Holy Grail of snowboarders for more than three decades: defying the laws of gravity …*

Right-hand page: *Leading by example: funboard and kiteboard legend Robby Naish plummeting through virgin powder in Chamonix.*

Jumping is great, landing safely even better. In competition mode, helmets and back protection are standard and de rigueur to help prevent injury.

Loners and **Followers** of the **Herd** ...

Alpine, freeride and freestyle are far and away the most important categories these days, although it must be said that the first two are progressively on their way out. Freestyle has emerged over the past few years as a cross-disciplinary phenomenon, no longer confined to snow parks but routinely practised in open terrain as backcountry snowboarding continues to grow in popularity. But freeriders still proclaim themselves defenders of the true snowboarding faith. As for manufacturers, they have quickly picked up on the cross-disciplinary trend and are turning out an increasing number of multipurpose boards. So-called 'cyberboarders' have a plethora of high-tech gadgetry at their disposal, ranging from the 'intelligent' snowboard to MP3 goggles and helmets with built-in hi-fi systems.

Alpine

Alpine addicts continue to carve, legs bent and hands touching the snow. Their bindings are steeply angled (40° minimum in competition), and their baseplates necessitate hard boots. The board itself is very narrow and even more wasp-waisted than ever. *Alpine disciplines* include parallel giant slalom (two side-by-side runs over two heats) and parallel slalom (same format but with gates spaced more closely together).

Left page: *Typical cyber-rider kitted out with an MP3 receiver in his breast pocket and a cordless Bluetooth kit around his neck.*

Right-hand page: *Ski-style snowboarding went Olympic as of 1998 despite mutterings of disapproval in some quarters.*

Following double-page spreads: *A successful freestyle figure: a powerful lift-off from the ramp followed by a minimum 360° upper-body rotation in mid-air and a clean landing on a steeply-angled slope.*

Freestyle

Freestylers execute airborne tricks and moves. They ride with their feet set further apart (in excess of 50 cm (1 foot 8 inches) between the two straps) and use broad, short, flexible boards and twin tips with soft boots and strap bindings set at a very open angle.

Freestyle disciplines include 'big air', 'halfpipe', 'slopestyle' (runs where competitors are judged on the basis of speed, jumps and style), and 'snowboardcross', where the winner is the first of four to six starters to complete a course dotted with moguls, ramps and tight curves.

Snowboardcross practitioners have lobbied long and hard to prevent the powers-that-be from robbing their discipline of its more spectacular elements. Here, the tracings are too flat and the course lacks cohesion.

Freeride

Freeriders wear soft boots and ride powder on long and wide rigid boards or twin tips (swallow-tail boards are making a comeback). The distance between bindings is important (50 to 55 cm [20 to 21.5 inches] and preferred angles vary from one snowboarder to the next but are generally 0 to 15° tail-side and 15 to 25° nose-side (other than for those who ride duck-footed). Purists tend to ride with bindings set slightly towards the rear of the board to facilitate disengaging.

Freeride disciplines include informal 'competitions' in optimal powder conditions, basically for the sheer fun of it. The freerider's first love is snowboarding with like-minded friends and, if there is a video camera around somewhere, then so much the better!

Right and following double-page spread: *Rite of initiation: flying the rocks. The pros jump anything up to twenty metres, but beginners are well advised to stick to shorter distances.*

Snowboarding Up Close

1 **Spoiler:** *rear part of the binding which supports the snowboarder when leaning back.*

2 **4 x 4 Disk:** *round section marked off in centimetres to facilitate screwdriver regulation of binding angles.*

3 **Nose:** *front end of the board.*

4 **Tail:** *rear end of the board.*

5 **Fixed Bindings:** *flexible bindings with hooked buckles.*

6 **Toe-Strap:** *used to secure toe.*

7 **Stance:** *distance between the feet on the board.*

Snowboard **Spin-Offs**

Kitesnowboarding – Mastering the Wind

For several years now, the white mountain ridges have taken on a splash of colour as kitesnowboarders take off and defy the laws of gravity. Kitesurfing, essentially a water-based discipline, first moved to its winter quarters in the mid-1990s. Dangling from 'wings' (kites) at the end of 25-metre- (80-foot-) long cords, riders initially took off on a number of exploratory jumps to experience wind conditions and currents. Then it dawned that the kite offered a whole new set of options, including riding big powder and either skimming over crests and rocks or going backcountry. The big plus with kitesnowboarding is that the kite pulls with next to no wind but also acts as a parachute and brake when travelling downhill.

As with its kitesurfing counterpart on water, kitesnowboarding presupposes respect for a few safety factors, notably avoiding areas with ravines and trees – not to mention high-tension cables.

Left, and right-hand page: A snowboard may offer limitless options, but the jump is far and away the favourite figure of adrenaline junkies.

Following double page spread: Steep-slope boarding Peruvian style. Since gliding on sand is tougher than on snow, it is essential to put on speed and lean back as far as possible. The snowskate may have a limited life span, but practitioners view it as a happy compromise between skating and snowboarding ...

Sandboarding – Riding the Dunes

Some say that sandboarding (sandsurfing) originated in the northeast of Brazil, whereas others swear blind it all started in California. There is also some confusion about *when* this snowboarding variant was launched: in the 1980s, certainly, but at the beginning or closer to the end of the decade? What is generally agreed, however, is that sandsurfing has taken off in South America (Peru, Chile), in Australia and in the United States. In effect, sandboarding can be practised anywhere there are stretches of steep dunes sufficiently long to string a few turns together. The hot spots at present include Merzuga in the Sahara, the Ica Desert and the Cerro Blanco in southern Peru, and Monument Valley in Colorado. The only sand *park* in the United States is currently the Sand Master Park in Oregon, a veritable sand dune ocean with all sorts of practice facilities based on skateboarding and snowboarding models.

As far as sandboarding equipment is concerned, there are no hard and fast guidelines. In Peru, riders use a handmade board secured by nails and waxed with candle grease. Where money is not so tight, however, a snowboard is used, more often than not with wakeboard-style bindings. Soft boots are acceptable, but basketball trainers are ideal.

Skatesnowboarding – Surfing the City

There could scarcely be a better illustration of how the city comes to the mountain and vice versa. Snowskateboarding is a compromise, a hybrid between skateboarding and snowboarding. Like the former, skatesnowboarding enables a rider to ride the urban landscape (ramps, stairs, etc.), move farther afield when snow falls on a resort and, not least, try out moves in a snow park. As in snowboarding, a rider can make small turns (although the pros have been known to ride the Grand Monets in Chamonix using a double-deck board). Although skatesnowboarding has a whole slew of plus points – no bindings, no ski passes, less risk of injury from a fall – and has been marketed aggressively, it has yet to live up to manufacturers' expectations.

Defying **Gravity**

Snowboarding has something of a split personality. Generations of adolescents may love its fun side, but it is also a formidable extreme sports discipline. Snowboarding has spawned its own brand of 'mutants', such as Jim Rippey, for example, a snowboarder and surfer who also happens to be the first man ever to have executed a back flip on a snowmobile!

The French have distinguished themselves on ultra-steep slopes. On 16 May 1986, Mont Blanc met its match when a group spearheaded by Bruno Grouvy became the first to descend by snowboard. Two years later, Gouvy successfully tackled the Eiger-Cervino-Jorasses triple and he was the first snowboarder at a height of 8,000 metres (26,250 feet), in the Himalayas. In 1986 also, Denis Bertrand, an extreme snowboarding pioneer who had cut his teeth alongside Gouvy on Mont Blanc, opted to snowboard down the northeast face of Les Courtes, part of the Mont Blanc massif – effectively covering the 'roof of Europe' in a single 24-hour period. Then, in 1995, Dédé Rehm and Jérôme Ruby, two snowboarders from Chamonix, were captured on film by photographer Philippe Fragnol as they took on a 60° run down the north face of Le Triolet. In 2001, another snowboarder from Chamonix – the diminutive Marco Siffredi – went one better: Mount Everest. Sadly, he was killed during his second attempt one year later, as were other intrepid snowboarders like Dédé Rehm and Bruno Gouvy. In their pursuit of the ultimate, they made the ultimate sacrifice and paid the ultimate price.

As for freestyle, the sky appears to be the limit. The best riders take on triple rotations and gaps can be anything up to fifty metres (165 feet) long. As for handrail figures in competition, they are truly phenomenal.

'Falling is not an option': top-flight snowboarders know that running a tight corridor is the ultimate challenge, where the slightest slip can prove fatal …

Chamonix snowboarders Jérôme Ruby and André-Pierre Rhem tackle the Mallory Run on the north face of the Aiguille du Midi. The valleys of the Mont Blanc massif are the ultimate playground for sheer-drop fanatics.

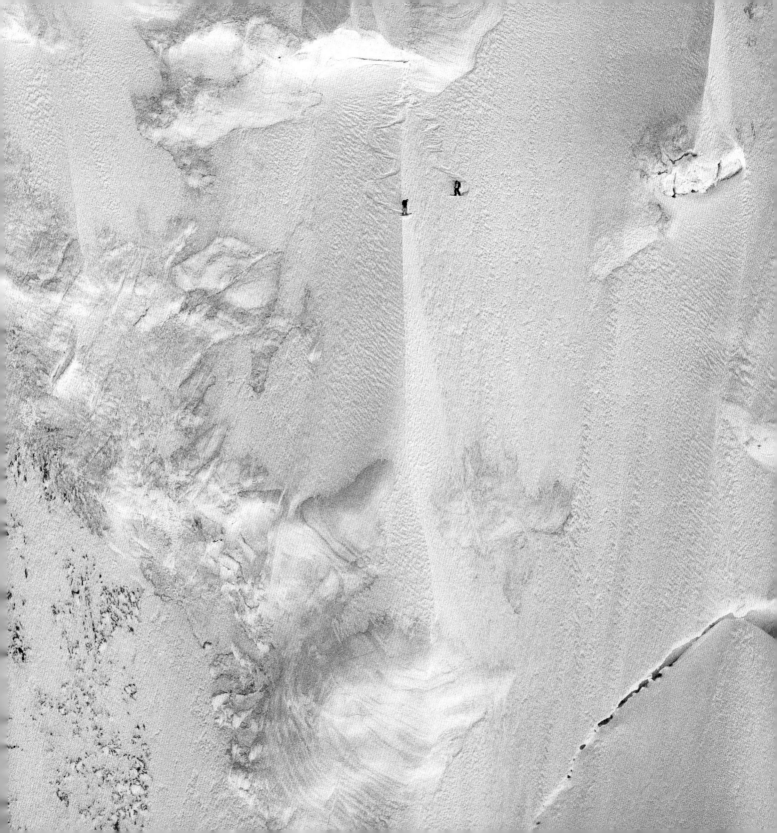

North face of Le Triolet, June 1995:
these vertiginous images of Rhem and
Ruby on their spectacular run made
headlines around the world.

*Extreme snowboarders Ruby and
Rhem in tandem once again, this
time on the south face of the Aiguille
du Moine.*

Ruby and Rhem yet again, this time
in the Macho Corridor on Mont
Blanc du Tacul above Chamonix.
The pair made the initial descent in
May 1994. Spring is the ideal season,
since melting snow makes for a
better grip on the near-perpendicular
slopes.

A question of technique: first man down checks out the quality of the snow and tests for potential avalanche conditions, then moves off line to allow the second man down. In a 50°-plus corridor like this, an ice axe is a must to dig in.

Running a corridor is akin to
mountaineering and, in practice,
the vast majority of practitioners
are seasoned mountain guides.
Potential risks and tricky passages
are identified during the ascent.

Bearing these and similar exploits in mind, each and every snowboarder asks the inevitable question: how far should I push it? In this regard, safety considerations are a two-edged sword. On the one hand, glossy resort brochures plug images of powder, the exhilaration of off-*piste* snowboarding and the availability of state-of-the-art equipment; on the other hand, flags are flown and areas cordoned off in a bid to dampen snowboarder ardour. To deal with what is clearly an untenable state of affairs, some resorts have come up with the concept of 'secure off-*piste* snowboarding'. This has its advantages, including virgin powder (if you're prepared to get up *really* early) and prompt access to medical or other intervention in the event of a mishap. However: zero risk equations are by no means to everyone's taste (other than the resort management).

The bottom line as far as safety is concerned boils down to common sense. There are certain basic rules when snowboarding freestyle, including appropriate head and back protection. In freeride, *never ever* venture off-*piste* on your own. *Always* check the weather forecast and *always* carry a rudimentary first-aid kit (various manufacturers worldwide have addressed this issue).

Jumping rock formations is part and parcel of the descent. On occasion, icy sections must be traversed by abseiling.

Right-hand page: Each turn must be carefully calculated and executed. The wall is unforgiving: 'Fall and you're dead'.

Les Arcs rider and Team Gros team member Vivien Dotti picks his way through powder in Canada, leaving a huge snowslide in his wake …

Right-hand page: Survival means staying on top. Research has shown that the avalanche balloon system prevents a snowboarder being buried in 96% of all cases …

Mountain Safety Glossary

ARVA. *A box that emits a sound when a rider is trapped under the snow; use in conjunction with a spade and a probe.*

Avalanche Ball. *A safety balloon attached to a cord remains on the surface, pinpoints the rider's location and facilitates rescue.*

Recco. *A reflector affixed to the boot helps locate a buried rider; works only in resorts equipped with detector devices, however.*

Avalung. *Air-sac device that enables the rider to breathe through a tube when buried under snow.*

ABS. *An airbag system with twin 75-litre balloons inflated via a ripcord-style ring.*

Leading **Light** of the **1980s**

For a decade and a half, Craig Kelly was the Burton stable's star performer, chalking up four world championship titles and three US Opens. But Craig pushed the envelope in other ways too, not least by committing himself and persuading others to commit to a sport whose athletes had, up to then, had little or no say in how things were run. Post-Craig, the majority of snowboard manufacturers bought into his vision of the sport.

In 2003, at the age of 36, Craig Kelly perished in an avalanche. He was a hero to a whole generation of riders and everyone who ever met or had dealings with him felt the same way about him – a sensational rider, a 'straight arrow', and a credit to the sport. After the glory years of competition, Craig had taken himself off to British Columbia, where he had worked as a guide, leading snowboard aficionados in search of virgin slopes. Terje Haakonsen, another snowboarding icon (see p. 92), had this to say about Kelly: 'When I first met him back in 1989 he was already my hero and my inspiration. I've never come across anyone since who could handle powder like Craig did, or who felt so passionately about the sport.'

Craig Kelly was an elegant rider and an indefatigable innovator, whose contribution to equipment development was matched only by his mental approach to snowboarding.

The **One** and **Only**

The moment of truth came in 1983 during the shooting of *Ski Espace* in Les Arcs. Jean Nerva, ski instructor, mono-skier and erstwhile music teacher from Villeurbanne, decided it was time to ring the changes. With his early Winterstick and his hiking boots wrapped in plastic shopping bags, Jean experienced for the first time the unbelievable feeling of floating through the snow. Together with his friend Mylène Duclos, Jean belonged to the band of 'harmless nutcases' who congregated in Grenoble, including Jean-Phi Garcia, Gilles Becker, Kébra, Jacques Gris, Kafi, and Gérard Rougier (later to be the long-serving president of the French Snowboarding Association).

Jean Nerva recalls those epic beginnings with undisguised delight: 'We were a crazy bunch, let me tell you. The Imperial Lizards. The Flying Carpets. Half the time we'd be walking back carrying a broken board. I remember the European Cup of 1986, where there was a double freestyle downhill – once with fins, then without. Sheer madness. I was riding with the Swiss boys (José Fernandes, Philippe Imhof and Antoine Massy), who'd turned up with Hooger Boogers – the first asymmetrical boards. State-of-the-art gear. They took the rest of us apart …'

Jean's professional career didn't really take off until he teamed up with the Burton stable: 'I had already negotiated a sportswear accessories deal with Oxbow and, when Burton came along, I had a whole ten thousand francs worth of sponsorship!' Then Jean met Peter Bauer and the pair went on to win competitions (among other things Nerva was moguls world champion in 1988) and make films, with scripts unlike anything around today. 1988 was a benchmark year, when Burton launched its first asymmetrical board, christened the 'PJ' in honour of Peter and Jean. Jean stopped competing in 1994, but he still rides and travels the world in search of spots.

Jean Nerva remains committed to snowboarding but, for some years now, he has been one of many notables who have gone back to conventional skiing.

The **Carver King**

'Carving' is usually defined as 'power and speed generated by leaning into the inside of the curve'. But Serge Vitelli imposed his own definition, in which a snowboarder lies flat on the *piste* while executing an optimally angled turn. Now that freestyle is all the rage, carving with your hand and nose touching the snow may seem a mite *passé* but, back in 1988 when Vitelli cut his first V-turn at the Club Med, his exploit hit the headlines in all the specialist media. All manner of possibilities opened up once he proved you could slice through the snow with a snowboard. Serge would go on to make his mark surfer-style, but, like every pioneer worth his salt, he started out on plates.

Following a successful career in competition interspersed with a couple of trips to the Cordilleras in the Andes, Serge joined forces with his lifelong friend Régis Rolland in a board-manufacturing venture that ultimately came good.

Vitelli spent his halcyon years with the Quiksilver Team before joining his close friend Régis Rolland at Apo.

All-Round **Showman**

Shaun Palmer's name is emblazoned on his torso in outsize letters and his snowboard sports the red, white and blue of the United States. He drives a vintage Cadillac, plays in a rock band with his Lake Tahoe buddies, dyes his hair yellow, red or green or simply shaves his head. But it would be a serious error of judgment to write him off as a snowboarder having a bad hair day or tag him with a 'bad boy' image.

The 1990s saw Palmer emerge as a 'zapper' of genius, the only rider to line up in four different disciplines at the winter X Games: snowboarding (where he has been a frontrunner for years), skiing, snow mountain-biking and snowmobile. The multitalented, multidisciplinary Palmer is an adrenaline junkie of the first order. Granted, his buzz is show rather than technique. In the pipeline now, it seems, is another gravity-defying ploy: freestyle motocross, would you believe?

Mister Palmer, like Jim Rippey, is one of the extrovert 'mutant' generation, able to turn his hand to every snow discipline imaginable.

Terje Haakonsen

Living **Legend**

Terje Haakonsen, born in 1974 in Aamot, Norway, couldn't wait to get enough cash to buy his first board, which he did at the age of thirteen. He spent days on end in the halfpipe and his technique came on in leaps and bounds, developing a few new moves of his own for good measure.

Jake Burton tipped Terje early on as the future of freestyle and, by the time he was fifteen, the young Norwegian was dominating the discipline with figures high above the halfpipe coping. Among them was the 'Haakon flip', a high aerial that involved approaching the wall backwards and executing a 720° rotation. Despite Terje's early success, he didn't rest on his laurels. Like his hero Craig Kelly, he developed a passion for freeride and soon started working on revolutionary board designs. There was more to come. Terje organised his own competition – the Arctic Challenge, held in Tromsö, Norway – a unique event designed by riders for riders that included skateboarding, freeride, dog-sledding, fishing and rock concerts. Significantly for snowboarding, this event saw the first experiments with super-halfpipes and quarterpipes. It was far removed from the Olympic Games Terje had boycotted in 1998.

Terje Haakonsen is a one-off, an exception who challenges every convention. Since April 2004, he has turned soccer pro and now plays for a team in the Norwegian third division !

Terje, snowboarder incarnate, riding not for glory but for the sheer pleasure of it – but always with that distinctive touch of class.

star in the **Alpine** Firmament

The blonde woman from Chamonix was destined to make history that day in Japan. The venue was Nagano, the year 1998. And 21-year-old Karine Ruby ascended the podium as the first-ever women's snowboarding world champion (giant slalom). She already had a clutch of victories to her credit and she would go on to notch up even more, including a string of world championship titles and World Cup victories by the bucketful. Inevitably, it seemed, she would emerge as the most-decorated woman athlete in alpine history.

When Karine ditched the slalom and opted for snowboardcross, the gold medals and crystal bowls kept on coming. She is a world-beater in every sense of the term — impetuous yet discreet. For Karine, medals don't matter as much as pushing herself to the limit and still having fun. That's the attitude that seems to prevail among French snowboarders, whose national squad has gone from one success to another, with frontrunners like Doriane Vidal (world halfpipe triple champion), Isabelle Blanc (Olympic parallel giant slalom winner in 2002) or Xavier De La Rue (double world champion in snowboardcross).

The Ruby family includes Olympic champion Karine and her brother, extreme descent specialist Jérôme.

Ruby

Karine

Changing of the **Guard**

'Getting up at six in the morning to go jogging and then wolfing down raw eggs all day long is not my thing,' says nineteen-year-old Shaun White. Scarcely. But White is no one-day wonder, no shooting star. Far from it, he is among the most innovative snowboarders around, what with his individualistic handrail slide moves and far-out tricks. A rebel *with* a cause, one might say.

Asked about the Olympics, Shaun simply shrugs. 'Can't say I've given them a second thought. If they happen, they happen, but I'm not gearing up for them.' Shaun is an exceptional skateboarder who competes for sheer fun, albeit at top-of-the-range competitions such as the Session-at-Vail, the X Games, the US Open and the Arctic Challenge. 'That's where the real action is,' he points out.

Shaun is a devil-may-care type, but there is a serious side to him. He is a hard-working student ('not just John Grisham novels') and a committed environmentalist. Longer term, he pictures himself as a marine biologist: 'If I could, I'd come back as a dolphin, freeing tuna fish from the nets and taking care of my other buddies in the sea'). By way of explanation, one might add that Shaun travels a lot by plane and tends to see large chunks of ocean on a regular basis …

Shaun is an exceptionally gifted snowboarder but, like his elder brother Terje, doesn't give a hoot for medals and awards. All he wants to do is stay cool … and ride …

Argentina

After every summer, several feet of powder snow fall in the Andes and snowboarders from around the globe congregate here to take advantage of the Argentine winter. Top resorts include Las Lenas, the classiest and most cosmopolitan, with the possibility of excursions from the Cajon Grande and La Hoya in Patagonia. The scenery and off-*piste* conditions are nothing short of magnificent.

Gliding in the Antipodean winter – an absolute must – not to mention a bit of snowkiting from time to time or a dip in a hot spring ...

Hotspots

Alaska

Between the Alaskan capital, Anchorage, and the freeride Mecca of Valdez, there is a territory one and a half times bigger than Switzerland, with a primeval valley that is glacier-free, unlike most other spots in Alaska. These virgin slopes are the ultimate destination for the dedicated freerider.

Régis Rolland navigating a 50° slope near Valdez. This is snowboarding at its most dedicated, although the danger of avalanches is less pronounced than in most massifs.

Canada

Blackcomb lies in British Columbia, about eighty miles from Vancouver, and is justly renowned for its off-*piste* vertical drops, its glaciers and its snow parks, which challenge even the most seasoned freestylers. Access is by helicopter and is comparatively cheap, no doubt because the competition is hotting up.

Oceans of powder spell beautiful jumps and excellent photo opportunities, although snow in the southern hemisphere has also been less in evidence in recent years.

France

As a rule, snowboarders steer clear of the Vallée Blanche and its twenty kilometres (twelve miles) of downhill runs, arguing that the terrain is too flat, especially towards the end of the run when you have to take the train back up in full gear (to avoid crevasses). A better option is to go for a more challenging location such as the Envers du Plan, where the slopes are steeper and largely uninterrupted by roads and walls.

The needle-like 3,842 metre-high Aiguille du Midi offers a stunning panorama over the roof of Europe and marks the departure point for an immense snowboarding landscape for seasoned pros and dedicated amateurs alike.

Kamchatka

Welcome to Kizimin in eastern Siberia, the world's most active volcanic region, a land where the mountains stretch as far as the eye can see and five-metre- (sixteen-foot-) thick blankets of snow beckon the serious snowboarder. Fly in and try out some of the beautiful downhill runs, including the one that starts on the massive hill opposite the towering 4,750-metre (15,500-foot) Klucevskaja Sopka, the highest volcanic peak in Europe and Asia. Here, the wind sends temperatures plummeting to -20° C (-4° F), the snow is black and the ice is like sheet metal: a lunar landscape where carbon particles settle on your clothing as you set off on your descent.

Glacial winds have sculpted the contours of the 2,470-metre-high Kizimin Peak, although the intrepid snowboarder can at least warm himself in the hot smoke and gases that escape from its crater!

Aeolian Islands

It takes three or four hours to climb the 923-metre (3,028-foot) volcanic-ash slopes of Stromboli for the privilege of a descent that resembles a sand dune run in the desert but offers the consolation of magnificent views over the Tyrrhenian Sea. If this doesn't appeal, then go for an easier option: the second-highest volcano in the archipelago is a more modest 491 metres (1,610 feet) high and is a sight easier to climb. And, if you're afraid your brand new parka might get dirty, then head for Lipari on the third island, where you can ski over a pumice stone mine!

When the snow wears thin on the volcanic slopes, there are always those that contrive to find a substitute riding solution ...

United States

For a taste of the Far West, head for Jackson Hole, Wyoming, which is not so much a ski resort as a cowboy town. Try horse-drawn skiing or snowboarding, then trade in your headgear for a Stetson and take a ride 3,185 metres (10,449 feet) up to Rendez-Vous Mountain, where one lift is earmarked for snowboarders. Snow quality is exceptional and descents are steep and often unmarked, with pronounced differences in levels of up to 1,200 metres (4,000 feet) in a single traverse.

It's advisable to keep a weather eye open for the ever-watchful snow patrols, the mountain 'cops' who are quick to intervene should one stray from the straight and narrow ...

Switzerland

The Valais boasts a multitude of ski resorts – more than sixty, ranging from the chic (Zermatt and Crans-Montana) to the more family-orientated, such as Nax or Orvonnaz, the latter known less for its slopes than for its thermal baths. Without exception, these resorts are natural snow parks. But for the snowboarding purist, the *only* place to go is Verbier, the European birthplace of freeride. Just picture it: four entire interlinked valleys with 500 kilometres (300 miles) of prepared slopes punctuated by myriad off-*piste* possibilities. The Barrage de Cleuson (aka 'Backside Mont-Fort'), with a mountain panorama that takes in Cervino, the Weisshorn and the Dent Blanche, is a must. Riding down through a totally unspoilt valley takes a full hour and, with a little bit of luck, you might even catch sight of the occasional ptarmigan or chamois.

A spectacle not to be missed: every year, the X-treme in Verbier brings together the best snowboarders of the day, who gather on the +/-55° downslopes on the north face of the Bec des Rosses.

Post-Revolutionary Decline?

Snowboard sales have stagnated as of late and there has been a move back to conventional skis. 'New School' skiing and its icons are currently attracting a new generation of enthusiasts. But snowboarding is far from being on the way out. It may have run its course for the time being, in part because it is well into its second genera-tion. Some thirty- and forty-year-olds who are essentially surfers at heart are returning to their first love, but youngsters are irresistibly drawn to the skateboarding parks, and it remains to be seen what will happen when they grow up. Suffice it to say, skiing will be only one option among many. Let's face it: snowboarding is here to stay.

Glossary

Aerial figure comprising a +/-100° rotation with the board before re-entering the pipe.

Air jump figure performed during competition.

Alpine refers to riders using carving boards, hard boots and plate bindings.

Angle regulates the position of the feet.

Back flip (dangerous) backwards jump.

Backside area on the slope behind a rider's back.

Baggy outsize, loose clothing.

Base underside of the board.

Baseless binding where the feet are in direct contact with the board.

Big Air see *Snow Parks on Parade*, page 39.

Bindings attachments used to secure a rider's feet to the board.

Boardercross (X) term derived from motocross; race competition where riders navigate jumps and banked turns.

Bone stylised figure completed with one leg straight and the other completely bent at the knee.

Carve execute a sweeping curve at optimal angle; presupposes use of alpine equipment (base plate).

Catch Tail jump figure with the board angled forward to the vertical and the tail grasped with the trailing hand.

Clickers step-in binding system manufactured by K2.

Coping halfpipe side wall.

Duck Foot stance where front binding is rotated towards the nose of the board and the back binding towards the tail, as opposed to both bindings being angled in the same direction, i.e., towards the nose.

Fakie backwards riding.

Fall Line invisible line that a snowball would take if rolled down a slope; 'snowboarding the fall line' refers to making turns along this imaginary line.

Fat as in 'go fat' (also 'big'); to perform a move or a discipline exceptionally well.

Flat even surface between two snow walls in a halfpipe.

Freecarving executing multiple turns in powder snow.

Freeride all-mountain off-*piste* snowboarding style including cruising, powder, jumps and trees.

Freestyle snowboarding style with accent on pipe and park riding and on tricks, switch-riding or fakies; requires shorter boards with soft boots.

Frontside area in front of a rider's toeside edge; a 'frontside spin' is where the rider turns into the spin frontside first (also known as 'toeside').

Gap jump figure with a space between take-off and landing.

Goofy-Footed right foot forward on the board (as opposed to 'regular-footed').

Grab jump figure where the rider holds the board with either hand while in the air; varieties of 'grab' include 'Indy', 'stalefish' and 'tail'.

Halfpipe a semi-tubular shape cut into the snow to facilitate tricks and jumps.

Handrail see *Snow Parks on Parade*, page 39.

Hard Boots rigid boots designed primarily for alpine disciplines.

Indy Grab grab manoeuvre where the centre of the board is clasped in the trailing hand.

Indy Nose Bone trick jump where the leg is extended backwards.

Indy Straight Legs trick jump where the legs are kept straight and the board is grasped between the rider's toes.

Inverted when a rider's head is below the level of the board.

Leash cord device attaching board to the rider's leg; often mandatory to prevent runaway boards.

Nose Leading (front) edge of a snowboard.

Nose Grab catching the leading edge (nose) during a jump.

Ollie skateboarding-style move where the rider jumps 'from the tail', i.e., using his back foot.

One Foot jump figure with one foot lifted from the board.

Pad piece of non-slip rubber mounted between the bindings; used to place the free foot securely when remounting a slope.

Park as in 'snow park': area at a winter sports resort maintained for snowboarding practice; complete with jumps, rails, halfpipes, etc.

Pizzas slang term for heavy flakes of snow (leading to powder conditions).

(Base) Plate as in 'plate binding'; designed for use with hard boots and alpine carving boards.

Regular-Footed left foot forward on the board (as opposed to 'Goofy-Footed').

Revert 180° vertical rotation.

Rider skiers *ski*, but snowboarders *ride* …

Rocket Air complex airborne manoeuvre with board held vertical, front hand grasping tip of board, front leg bent, back leg straight.

Shape board configuration (symmetrical, asymmetrical, directional, twin tip, etc.).

Slopestyle competition where riders take turns to go through a series of jumps and other obstacles (big air, halfpipe, handrails) while performing various tricks.

Snow Park see **Park**.

Soft Boots as the name suggests, not rigid like 'hard' boots.

Spin pivot on the board.

Spoiler rear binding support.

Spot snowboarding destination ('hot spot') or practice area.

Stance refers to the foot position created when bindings are mounted on a board, and also the specifications, like widths and angles.

Step-In automatic binding system; as opposed to strap bindings.

Stiffy slang term for straight leg jump.

Superpipe larger, wider and higher than a typical halfpipe; used progressively in competition.

Swallow shaped board tail for powder snow conditions.

Switch in general terms, to change ride direction; 'riding switch' for a goofy-footer means riding with the left foot forward as opposed to the right.

Table flat section between take-off and landing.

Tail trailing end of a snowboard (as opposed to the Nose).

Tail Bone jump figure where the trailing leg is extended.

Tail Grab jump figure with tail grasped by either hand.

Tombstone halfpipe take-off ramp.

Traverse to cut across the fall line.

Twin Tip board with identically shaped nose and tail; used predominantly in freestyle riding.

Vert (Vertical) section of a halfpipe wall that is at a 90° angle to the flat.

Wall snow lining each side of a halfpipe; a 'wall trick' is performed using the contours of the halfpipe.

Wipe-Out fall; crash.

180° a 180° airborne spin landing in the opposite direction of travel; also known as a 'half cab'.

3-6 or **360°** jump figure in which the rider twists 360° in the air and lands facing the same direction as take-off.

540° jump figure involving one and a half body twists.

720° jump figure in which two full body twists are completed.

1080° jump figure in which three full body twists are completed.

Appendices

Further Reading

Practical guides

Where to Ski and Snowboard 2005 Chris Gill ed., Nortonwood Publishing, 2004.

The Good Skiing & Snowboarding Guide ('Which?' Guides) Peter Hardy, Felice Hardy, Which? Books, 2004.

Illustrated Guide to Snowboarding Kevin Ryan, Masters Press 1999.

Snowboard. Les plus beaux hors-pistes Jean Nerva, Glénat, 2001.

Snowboard: 256 figures (with CD-ROM), L. Durieux, Association française de snowboard, Amphora, 2000.

2005 World Snowboard Guide Stephen Dowle, revised, 2004.

Snowboard: Your Guide to Freeriding, Pipe & Park, Jibbing, Backcountry, Alpine, Boardercross and More Joy Masoff, School & Library Binding, 2003.

The Snowboard Guide Europe Alex Reiser, Jason Horton, Remedy Publishing, 2002.

The Complete Snowboarder Jeff Bennett, Charles Arnell, Scott Downey, International Marine Publishing, 2000.

Backcountry Snowboarding Christopher Van Tilburg, Mountaineers Books, 1998.

The Snowboard Book: A Guide for All Boarders Lowell Hart, W.W. Norton & Company Ltd., 1997.

Equipment

Snowboards: From Start to Finish Tanya Lee Stone, Blackbirch Press, 2000.

Filmography

Apocalypse Snow, Trilogy (Régis Rolland)

Cannon surf 1 et 2 (Apocalypse vidéo)

Pachamama (Jean Nerva/Burton)

Le Jouet (Jean Nerva/Sony)

Dropstitch (Chunkiknit)

Fast food (Alterna Action films)

First Step Basix Tricks (411 Productions)

Kevolution (Cinemaseoane)

Les Nuits de la glisse (www.nuitdelaglisse.com)

Lost in Transition (Standard films)

Love and Hate (Kid and snow productions)

The Shaun White Album (Cinemaseoane)

Five To Nine (Sound straight productions)

KingPin Greatest Hits (Kingpin Production)

Everyday Something (Neoproto Films)

Pop (Hot snowboard video)

Promo Copy (Hot snowboard video)

Most of the films listed below may be ordered directly from:
www.x-tremevideo.com/;
http://www.actionsportsvideos.com/;
amazon. com and www.advd.tv/.

Snowboarding on the Web

www.abc-of-snowboarding.com
www.agoride.com
www.boardtheworld.com
www.freecarve.com
www.onboardmag.com
www.powderroom.net
www.rideculture.com
www.ridespirit.com
www.skipass.com
www.snowboard-city.com
www.snowboard-life.com
www.snowboardermag.com
www.snowboarding.com
www.snowboarding2.com
www.snowboardjournal.com
www.snowboard.mountainzone.com
www.transworldsnowboarding.com
www.worldsnowboardguide.com

Acknowledgements

The author would particularly like to thank:
Jacques Benayoun (Morozzo agency),
Rémy Fière, Philippe Fragnol,
Jean Nerva, Régis Rolland.

Photographic credits

Pascal Boulgakow 8–9, 22 mr, 23 tl, 23 tr, 26 t, 28–29, 32, 33 tr, 37, 39, 48–49, 50–51, 51, 52–53, 60, 61, 82 tl, bl, br, 95, 98–99.

Jake Burton 14, 15, 17, 83 t, b, 96-97, 97.

Jean-Marc Favre cover and flap 1, cover and flap 4, 10, 12–13, 16, 20, 21, 22 tl, 22 bl, 23 m, 23 br, 24–25, 30, 33 tl and bl, 34 l, 35, 42, 44–45, 47, 54, 55, 56, 57, 78, 86–87, 89.

Philippe Fragnol cover and flap 2, cover and flap 3, 3, 4–5, 6–7, 18, 19, 22–23 b, 22 tm, 27, 31, 40–41, 43, 64–65, 66, 67, 68, 69, 70, 71, 72, 73, 74, 75, 76, 77, 79, 80, 82 tr, 83 m, 85, 90–91, 100, 101, 104, 105, 114–115.

Getty images *Melissa McManus* 106–107.

Manu/Arc en ciel 36, 38, 108–109.

Luc Monnet 58–59.

Rapsodia *Laurent Bouvet* 26 b, 102, 103, 110–111, 112–113 – *Christian Haase* 62–63.

Jean-Michel Schmetz 81.

Jean-François Vibert 1.

DR 24, 33 br, 34 r, 46, 49, 63, 93.

Moore